BIBLE READING

Also by Michael Green

Baptism
Closer to Jesus
The Empty Cross of Jesus
Evangelism for Amateurs
Evangelism through the Local Church
Freed to Serve
How Can I Lead a Friend to Christ?
I Believe in the Holy Spirit
I Believe in Satan's Downfall
New Life, New Lifestyle
Who is this Jesus?
Why Bother with Jesus?
You Must Be Joking!

Bible Reading
for Amateurs

Michael Green

Hodder & Stoughton
LONDON   SYDNEY   AUCKLAND

This book is a small tribute to the great work of the International Bible Society and the British and Foreign Bible Society in helping total amateurs to fall in love with the greatest story ever written.

Illustrations © 1999 by Taffy Davies
Copyright © 1999 by Michael Green

First published in Great Britain in 1999

British Library Cataloguing in Publication Data
A record for this book is available from the British Library

ISBN 0 340 74540 1

Typeset by Avon Dataset Ltd, Bidford-on-Avon, Warks

Printed and bound in Great Britain by
Clays Ltd, St Ives plc

Hodder and Stoughton Ltd
A Division of Hodder Headline
338 Euston Road
London NW1 3BH

Contents

Introduction

The world's best-seller

The Bible is far and away the world's best-seller, not just in the West but all over the world. In the days of the USSR people would risk their lives to obtain a copy. It is so powerful that today many countries ban its entry, fearful of the impact it will make. Wherever it is taken seriously it transforms lives for the better. A truly amazing book.

But the man in the street is profoundly ignorant of it. He never reads it. It's a remarkable thing, but he's embarrassed by it.

And yet our culture has been shaped more by this book than any other single influence.

The story of the Bible is constantly being retold in historical novels, like Frederick Buechner's *The Son of Laughter* on the life of Jacob, or the best-selling Brazilian author Paulo Coehlo's *The Fifth Mountain* on the life of Elijah, or Thomas Cahill's *The Hinges of History* – a detailed retelling of events in the Old Testament.

The same is taking place in film and television. A film like *Amistad* is dominated by the Bible. Steven Spielberg's *Prince of Egypt* is an animated portrayal of the life of Moses, while the story of Jesus comes from director after director. Think of Zeffirelli's *Jesus*, or the Canadian film *Jesus of Montreal*. The film-makers cannot resist his fascination.

Funny thing, isn't it? The level of Bible knowledge in home and school is almost nil. The Christian Church seems to keep its treasure very much to itself (in a church building, on a Sunday). Its members for the most part do not read it. And yet in the culture at large it remains the most powerful story in the world.

What is this book? What is the secret of its staying power and fascination? How can we get into it and experience its impact? This little volume is designed to enable complete amateurs in Bible knowledge to discover its riches for themselves. We think of the word 'amateur' as a non-professional of some kind, someone who isn't paid for doing his thing. But the root meaning of the word is 'lover'. I have come to love the Bible, and I hope this little book will turn some of you, too, into lovers of the greatest story ever told. Read on!

1

What is the Bible?

Not a book, but a library

The word 'Bible' comes from a Greek word meaning 'books', and that gives us a clue to start off with. We are not dealing with a single book, but with a library. The Bible does in fact consist of no fewer than sixty-six books. Some are long, some short. They were written over a period of more than a thousand years in three languages, Hebrew, Greek and Aramaic. They had astonishingly varied authors, from shepherds to kings, poets to historians, prophets to warriors, mystics to fishermen.

Its unity

If you got a bunch of people as various as that into a room and asked them their views on God and man, lifestyle and destiny, you would get as many answers as there were people. But the truly remarkable thing about the Bible, which justifies us in naming it a single book, is that you find a common understanding, a unified teaching running right through it.

Always you get the same picture of *God*. He is the one and only author of life, the only proper object of worship. He is personal, but beyond personality. The male and female together represent something of his being. He is the source of all morality, perfect and pure and just. He is full of love for the world he has created and the people he has brought into being. The true God whom the Bible brings before us is the utterly loving but utterly incorruptible Creator.

We find, to our amazement, that we get a common understanding of *human nature* running through all the books of the Bible. Human beings are not gods, as some New Agers like Shirley MacLaine would have it. We are not just sophisticated animals, as some of the biologists maintain, or chemical constructs in motion, as some behaviourists believe. We are neither naked apes nor little angels, but made in his image, with the ability to speak, to pray and to know the difference between right and wrong. God intended us to live in families and enjoy his company. But almost every page of the Bible reflects the fact that all down the ages human beings have rejected that ideal. We have gone our own way, not God's way. We have pleased ourselves, not God. We have left God out of our lives and paddled our own canoe. And the chaos in human affairs all springs from that basic attitude of rebellion and disobedience. It is not just the times that are out of joint: we are. Now that is a very radical understanding of human nature, and very unfashionable (although every edition of the Sunday papers underlines its truth!). But it is the view on which the biblical writers are unanimous.

There is another major theme, consequent upon

these two, which binds the whole Bible together. It is *rescue*, restoration. The Bible writers often call it salvation. 'Save' is not a word we use much nowadays, but think of someone being saved from drowning or from a burning building and you will get the idea. Both drowning and burning suggest mortal danger. That is how the Bible understands the consequences of our human rebellion. Our predicament is serious. And God might well have washed his hands of us and started again, as D.H. Lawrence advised him to! But no. The Bible writers all maintain that God cares about us so much that he has found a costly way to restore us to his company and rescue us from the mess into which our self-centredness has plunged us. This is a remarkable insight. In other faiths you find a God who is a stern judge, or who does not care about human beings, or who is impersonal or sadistic. The Bible tells us that God loves us so much that he was determined to do something to rescue us from the guilt our actions and attitudes bring upon us and from the grip in which our failures imprison us.

In a word, the great theme of the Bible is 'God to the rescue' (that, in fact, is the meaning of the name 'Jesus'). God is the Saviour, the one who comes to restore the situation which we have messed up. The centrepiece of the whole story is the mind-boggling claim that God came in person to this earth as Jesus. He lived a matchless life, and offered that life up voluntarily on the cross as the incredibly costly way of removing our guilt, breaking our chains and making possible a way back to companionship with God. This is no mere journey from the alone to the Alone. It involves human beings in a new community who love and seek to advance the claims of God in this world.

As if that was not enough, the Bible writers are confident that there is a *future* awaiting the people of God. He cares for us so much he will not scrap us when we get old and die. He offers us a welcome in his home in heaven. Our destiny is not to go out like a light, not to be condemned to a ceaseless round of reincarnation, but to know and enjoy for ever the God who loved us and gave himself for us, and to do so in the company of all who love him and have looked to him for rescue.

That is the kernel of what the Bible is about. It would have been amazing if one person had had such improbable insights. There is no example of any single person ever coming up with anything comparable. But when all the forty or so authors of the Bible agree in this view of God, man, evil, restoration, the new community and human destiny, it is simply staggering. No wonder the Bible writers claimed, and Christians have always recognised, that they were inspired. We shall look at this more closely in a later chapter. God himself gave these insights to the writers. They could never have come up with the same answers all by themselves.

So despite the many centuries over which this library of the Bible was written, despite its many authors and different languages, there is a remarkable unity which holds it all together. We have every right to see it as 'the book' rather than a stray collection of books embodying merely human ideas.

The library with two shelves

This library of the Bible has two main halves, called the Old Testament and the New Testament. The word 'testament' means 'covenant' or 'agreement', and the first part of the Bible enshrines the Old Covenant God established with his people before he came to our world in Jesus Christ. The New Covenant is the story of that coming and its significance. It brings to a climax God's self-disclosure.

To put it another way, the Old Testament is all about promise, and the New is all about fulfilment. If the Old Testament records what 'God spoke in the past to our forefathers through the prophets', the New tells us how God has 'spoken to us by his Son', in whom all the older revelation was summed up, confirmed and transcended (Hebrews 1:1–2).

Just a further word of explanation to help us find our way around this large book. *The Old Testament* falls into three main parts, called the Law, the Prophets and the Writings. The Law comprises the first five 'books of Moses'. The Prophets fall into two divisions: the 'former prophets', made up of Joshua, Judges, Samuel and Kings, and the 'latter prophets', comprising Isaiah, Jeremiah, Ezekiel and a collection of twelve shorter prophecies. The Writings contain the rest of the Old Testament, and are generally later than the Law and the Prophets.

If you think it is a bit odd to find historical books like Kings included in the Prophets, the answer is rather interesting. God reveals himself throughout the whole Old Testament period in two main ways, by mighty works (like the Exodus) and by prophetic words. The two belong together. God's mighty deeds of rescue and judgment would not have been intelligible unless they were interpreted by the prophets, God's 'spokesmen' who received and passed on his message. This interplay of mighty deed and prophetic word in the Old Testament explains why history and prophecy are so intermingled in its pages, and why the historical books can be seen as prophetic.

The New Testament falls naturally into four. There are first of all the four Gospels, recording the story of Jesus, whose life is not only God's crowning revelation to man, but mankind's perfect response to God. His coming, life, teaching, death and resurrection are brought powerfully before us in the Gospels, which were themselves an entirely new form of literature.

Then comes the Acts of the Apostles, the story of how the first Christians spread across the known world in thirty years. It makes thrilling reading. It is followed by the epistles or letters from the first Christian leaders, some to individuals and some to churches. These reflect on the significance of Jesus and the implications he has for the Christian community. Finally there is a highly pictorial book, Revelation, lifting our hearts to grasp something of God's future.

So the Old Testament records the witness of those who were, consciously or unconsciously, reaching forward to God's full revelation in Jesus Christ, while the New Testament records the witness of those who saw and heard him when he was on earth, and who proclaimed far and wide the good news of who he was and what he had done for mankind. That is what the Bible is about. It's the library with a single great theme.

2

What can it do for me?

What's in it for me?

'What's in it for me?' is a very natural question, particularly in today's fast-moving society when we are too busy to bother with anything that does not have some immediate relevance. So no wonder people ask that question about Bible reading. 'What's the point?' 'What can it do for me?'

It can do a great deal.

What it did for some sceptics

Years ago there was a young French scholar called Émile Caillet who was determined to discover truth. So he turned to philosophy, and he spent some ten years studying all the philosophical systems that had ever been devised. He was disappointed with what he found. So he said, 'I will write my own philosophy,' – and he did. However, when he looked back over it some time later, he was again disappointed with what he had written. He despaired of ever finding truth.

One day he came home and found his wife reading

the Bible. 'Get that book of superstition out of my house,' he roared. She refused. Instead, she pleaded with him to at least glance at its contents. With a bad grace he did. And he was entirely captivated by what he read. Here was the teaching which had so long eluded him, and which immediately convinced him of its truth. He became a Christian. In due course his biblical studies led him into becoming a theologian. Indeed, he spent many fruitful years as a professor at Princeton. Looking back on the whole experience, he said, 'At last I have found a book which understands me.'

The Bible has always had this life-changing power. In the early days of the Church a very able intellectual, Justin, was treading much the same path as Émile Caillet. He had studied the Platonic, Aristotelian and Cynic philosophical systems of the ancient world, and like Caillet he was disappointed because none of them had that ring of truth about them that he was looking for. One day he met an old man in the fields, who, seeing his philosopher's cloak, asked him what the true philosophy was. Justin was, of course, unable to give a satisfactory reply, because he had not found it himself. So the old man asked him to read and reflect on a copy of the scriptures. Justin was reluctant to examine these 'barbaric writings'. But he did, and he was never the same again. For he found that the scriptures 'possess a terrible power in themselves' and also 'a wonderful sweetness' which made an indelible impression on him. He became a follower of Jesus, and refused to lay aside his philosopher's cloak but fearlessly proclaimed the 'true philosophy' he found in the scriptures throughout his life, until he was dragged off to a martyr's death. He saw those same scriptures lead his pupil Athenagoras to Christ. Both of them figure among the major Christian thinkers of the second century. Both of them were won by the powerful truth they found in the scriptures. The Bible is a life-changing book. *That* is what it can do for you!

When Charles Darwin first visited the Galapagos Islands on the *Beagle* he found that the inhabitants were utterly dejected and corrupt. He was very depressed by their abysmal condition. When he went back years later, after the first missionaries had brought the scriptures there, he was so fascinated by the transformation of the people that he became a lifelong subscriber to the Bible Society!

Charles Dickens put the matter very succinctly: 'The New Testament is the best book the world has ever known and will ever know.' 'It is more than a book to me,' reflected Napoleon, on St Helena. 'It is, as it were, a person.' It has this astonishing power to address us personally, as if it were written for us alone. 'It is talking to me and about me,' said the Danish philosopher, Søren Kierkegaard. Perhaps that is why no sceptical criticism, no persecution, no confiscation, no sanctions against reading this book have ever succeeded. Its sales just go on growing: there is no other book in the same league.

But let's be specific. What can it do for me?

What can it do for me?

First and foremost, *it can change your life*. Not that it has any magical powers, but it puts you in touch with

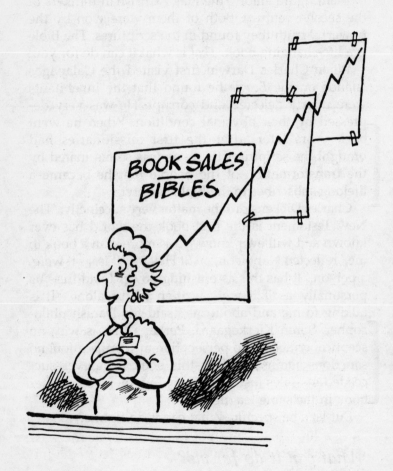

the living God who can give you spiritual life just as he has given you natural life. The written word can put you in touch with Jesus the living word (or self-disclosure) of God. Just as you can only know my unseen thoughts if I clothe them in words, so we can only know the unseen God if he communicates to us in words we can take in. That he has done. As the American preacher D.L. Moody put it, 'The Bible was not given to increase our knowledge. It was given to change our lives.'

Once people start reading it with an open heart, God is able to get through to them. St John's Gospel embodies that claim very clearly. He tells us why he wrote his book. It is so 'that you may believe that Jesus is the Christ, the Son of God, and that by believing you may have life in his name' (John 20:31).

Notice the two stages in that purpose. The first one is calculated to show the reader what John himself discovered by personal companionship with Jesus – that he really is the Son of God. John gives us in his Gospel seven great signs which Jesus did, followed by the supreme sign of his death and resurrection. These convinced John himself, and he records them for others so that they may see solid grounds for belief. But it can never rest there. Jesus is the one who gives a new dimension to life, a spiritual rebirth, no less. That is what John wants for his readers – that they may have 'life in his name'. Had not Jesus proclaimed, 'I have come that they may have life, and have it to the full' (John 10:10)?

There are many other things that the Bible can do for us. Once we have discovered the new life in Christ, scripture *is able to build us up* and show us more and more of the treasures we have inherited as Christians (Acts 20:32). It is a gradual process. We are not dropped into the deep end all at once. There are lots of things we shall not understand. But there is plenty that we can readily take on board and find really nourishing – particularly in the Gospels and Psalms. The Bible calls itself milk, milk for babies in the Christian life. St Peter writes to new believers, 'Like newborn babies, crave pure spiritual milk, so that by it you may grow' (1 Peter 2:2). Of course, we are not meant to stay at that level for long, but to develop. Wouldn't it be disappointing if a nursing baby never got on to solid food? Accordingly, the Bible also compares itself to meat for those who are mature. St Paul has reason to complain of some of the Christians at Corinth whom he had himself led to Christ, 'I gave you milk, not solid food, for you were not yet ready for it. Indeed, you are still not ready' (1 Corinthians 3:2). Alas, that is true of so many Christians today. They are semi-starved. They have not been built up in their spiritual lives by the scriptures.

The Bible *gives us a deep insight into Jesus himself*, and there is no substitute for that. Hear Dr Christopher Chavasse, a saintly bishop of Liverpool in days gone by.

The Bible is the portrait of our Lord Jesus Christ. The Gospels are the figure itself in the portrait. The Old Testament is the background leading up to the divine figure, pointing towards it and absolutely necessary to the composition as a whole. The Epistles serve as the dress and equipment of the figure, explaining and describing it. Then, while by our Bible reading we study the portrait as a whole, the miracle happens and the figure comes to life. Stepping down from the canvas of the written word, the everlasting Christ of the Emmaus story becomes himself our Bible teacher, to interpret to us in all the scriptures the things concerning himself.

That may be language of sixty years ago, but the meaning is both clear and helpful. Luther put it in a memorable way, 'As we come to the cradle only to find the baby, so we come to the scriptures only to find the Christ.'

The Bible's own claims

The Bible itself contains some marvellous images of what it can do. It is like a *fire*, to warm our hearts when they are cold. ' "Is not my word like fire," declares the Lord, "and like a *hammer* that breaks a rock in pieces?" ' (Jeremiah 23:29). I don't know about you, but my heart is often both cold and rock-like. I need to have that rock broken up, that fire lit up! That is what scripture can do when we come to it humbly.

And here is something else. It is described as the *sword* which the Holy Spirit uses to fight for us in times of temptation (Ephesians 6:17). The classic example of this, of course, is the use Jesus himself made of some verses he seems to have committed to memory from the book of Deuteronomy. Do you remember how, when fiercely tempted in the wilderness, he faced each temptation with 'It is written . . .' (Matthew 4:1–11)? In each case that 'sword of the

Spirit' drove the tempter away. Try it. It works!

No wonder the prophet Ezekiel sees that portion of the scriptures which was written in his day as something *wonderfully sweet*. 'He said to me, ". . . eat this scroll that I am giving you and fill your stomach with it." So I ate it, and it tasted as sweet as honey in my mouth' (Ezekiel 3:3). Bizarre imagery, perhaps, but wonderfully clear teaching! The psalmist, too, is so thrilled with God's word through the scriptures that he creates an elaborate psalm, every verse of which sings of one of the splendours of God's revelation. And that, by the way, is Psalm 119, the longest psalm in the book. He certainly found it sweet and nourishing to his soul, and so will we if only we will start reading a bit of it on a daily basis. It will build us up, and be 'a lamp to our feet and a light to our path' (Psalm 119:105). We all need a bit of illumination and guidance in the problems that beset us daily, and you will be amazed to find that in your daily reading you often get just the insight and direction that you were looking for.

John Wesley certainly discovered the truth of this, and it might be good to end this chapter with his passionate outburst:

> I want to know one thing, the way to heaven. God himself condescended to teach that way. For this very end he came from heaven. He has written it down in a book. O give me that book, at any price, give me that book! If I have it, there is knowledge enough for me. Let me be a man of one book!

3

How shall I approach it?

What is the Bible for?

There used to be a book on my shelves called *The Bible as Literature*. I do not have it any longer! You see, the Bible is magnificent literature. It is the greatest literature in the world, and the old King James version is a highlight of English prose (which is why agnostic men of letters are so keen to retain it). But it was not designed to be read or valued simply for its literary quality.

There still is a book on my shelves entitled *The Bible as History*. I have not disposed of it during my various house moves for two good reasons. It has a lot of valuable material in it, and the Bible *is* historically reliable. Every discovery in archaeology vindicates the accuracy of the biblical account. But the Bible is not primarily intended to be a history book. It contains history, but it is much more than that.

There is a third way of looking at the Bible that is very common. It is seen as *inspirational*. It gives us inspiring thoughts from spiritually gifted human beings about God and the good life. To be sure, it was written by people in close touch with God, and it does

17

tell us a lot about how life should be lived. But that is not what the Bible is about. It is not the product of inspiring people. It is not comparable to inspiring masterpieces like Shakespeare's *Hamlet* or Handel's *Messiah*. It claims to be, with very good reason as we shall see in a later chapter, 'breathed out' by God. He breathed out the material we have in the Bible, and a variety of human authors were sufficiently in touch with God to assimilate it and write it down for the benefit of mankind. In a letter to his friend Timothy, St Paul says, 'From infancy you have known the holy Scriptures, which are able to make you wise for salvation through faith in Christ Jesus. All Scripture is God-breathed and is useful for teaching, rebuking, correcting and training in righteousness, so that the man of God may be thoroughly equipped for every good work' (2 Timothy 3:15–17). *That* is what the Bible is for. It is revelation breathed out by God, not bright ideas about God dreamed up by man. It is God's self-disclosure, not man's speculation.

As such it is immensely profitable. Profitable for teaching us about God and about life, for rebuking us when we need it, for correcting us when we have gone wrong, and for training us in the Christian life so that we may go deep, and become mature and a blessing to society.

Very well, if that is why God gave us the Bible, it suggests to me a number of important attitudes I need to adopt as I come to read it.

How shall I approach it?

First, I shall want to approach it *humbly*. If scripture really is designed by God to teach us what we need to know about him, for our good and the good of others, then it is obvious that you and I must come to it humbly. Some Christian leaders in the New Testament are charmingly described as 'servants of the word'. That is the right attitude. I am not *over* it, to judge it and decide what bits I shall accept and what bits I can reject. I am *under* the word. I need to let it judge me if necessary. I need to listen reflectively to what it is saying and see how it applies to my life. It is astonishing how blind some highly intelligent but proud people can be to what the Bible is saying to them. It is equally astonishing to see the spiritual insight gained by utterly uneducated people who come humbly to the scriptures, saying, in effect, 'Speak, Lord, for your servant is listening.' St Augustine came to recognise that the scriptures are 'letters from home'. But he had not always seen them in that light. Before his conversion, he tells us, he was dissatisfied with pagan philosophers like Cicero and resolved to turn to the Bible in search of wisdom. 'But I did not understand it, because I came with pride. The Bible is a book for those who come to it humbly.' That is how I need to approach it.

Second, I need to come *expectantly*. Most of all I want to meet the living word within the written word. I want to meet Christ in the pages before me. It is rather like a correspondence between a pair of lovers. When she gets a letter from him, she reads it eagerly, mulling over words and suggestions. She reads it again, commits bits of it to heart. It is not the letters on the page that thrill her, but the person of her lover which those letters bring to her. Bible reading can be deadly dull if you read it as history, literature or bright ideas about God from religious people. But it becomes as thrilling as any love letter when you seek to meet your Lord in its pages.

One of the most remarkable spiritual leaders in the mid-twentieth century is Archbishop Anthony Bloom. A Russian *émigré*, he was aggressively anti-Christian in his youth. He hated the very idea of God. Indeed, convinced that life had no meaning, he was contemplating suicide. And then one day he was forced to listen to a Christian priest. It made him furious, and he went home to read one of the Gospels in order to prove the man wrong. He selected Mark, because it was the shortest. He tells us, 'Before I reached the third chapter I suddenly became aware that on the other side of my desk there was a presence. And the certainty was so strong that it was Christ standing there that it has never left me. This was the real turning point.' He became successively a doctor, a priest and an archbishop, but it all began when he met Christ himself in the pages of the Gospel. He was not expecting anything of the sort at the time – but he has been ever since, and so should we.

Third, I must approach the Bible *honestly*. I shall find difficulties that I cannot explain. Sometimes they will be intellectual difficulties, like how Jesus could be both Son of God and a human being. Sometimes philosophical difficulties, like the possibility of miracles. Sometimes moral difficulties, especially in the Old Testament where God commanded the Jews to slaughter the Amalekites who could infect them with idolatry and immorality.

So I suggest you keep a Pending Tray! Put problems like that in the tray, and talk them over, when opportunity offers, with some wise Christian friend who knows more than you do. Don't let what you *don't* understand ruin what you *do* understand, or you will gain no profit from your Bible reading.

Suppose you were served a beautifully cooked trout for your meal, would you carefully separate the bones from the flesh – and then struggle to swallow the bones, while leaving the flesh aside? Of course not. You would put the bones on the side of the plate and tuck into the meat. Do that with your Bible reading. But never be obscurantist. Never pretend to yourself that there are no real problems. Do not leave them unexamined. You have to handle the Bible with the utmost intellectual honesty. But do not allow your devotional time with the Bible to be spoiled because you are gnawing away at the bones rather than feasting on the flesh. Keep the bones until later.

It is wise to come to the Bible *imaginatively*. I sometimes try to put myself into the shoes of someone I have just read about in the story. If it is a passage from the Gospels, I try to recapture what it must have felt like when Jesus fed five thousand people from a few small loaves. What would I have written in my diary when I staggered back home, footsore but awestruck, at the end of such a day? Or I wonder how I would have reacted to hearing the letter to the Philippians for the very first time as the messenger, Epaphroditus, sweating from his long journey, read it aloud to our

Christian group packed into a house in the garrison town of Philippi.

Please note that I am not advocating wild, uncontrolled flights of fancy – they can lead you all over the place! But I am encouraging you to allow your God-given imagination to engage with the biblical text. It will help to make your Bible reading spring to life.

Fifth, I shall want to read the Bible *attentively*. It is no good rushing into a hastily chosen Bible passage, spinning through it, and expecting to get something from it. That would be as useless as seeing a nice meal on your plate and sparing time only to lick the gravy or grab a potato on the run! I need to make time to read, and then to read the same piece again more slowly, and allow the Lord to make something come alive for me.

You know how it is at Christmas in the High Street. There are coloured bulbs up everywhere. You hardly notice them in the daytime. They look dull and useless. But when they are switched on in the evening, it is entirely different. God will switch on the lights for us and make some thought from the scripture luminous to us, if we take time in his presence, read attentively and ask him to meet with us.

Sixth, I need to approach the Bible *obediently*.

Do not merely listen to the word, and so deceive yourselves. Do what it says. Anyone who listens to the word but does not do what it says is like a man who looks at his face in a mirror, and after looking at himself, goes away and immediately forgets what he looks like. But the man who looks intently into the perfect law that gives freedom, and continues to

do this, not forgetting what he has heard, but doing it – he will be blessed in what he does. (James 1:22– 5)

A good point, isn't it? You would never dream of looking at your face in the mirror, see a great smudge, and do nothing about it. You would act. You would wipe it off. That is what you and I are meant to do when we read a bit of scripture. We need to apply it to our lives, and act.

Finally, I must come to it *regularly*. I do not look in the mirror once a week and hope that all will be well the rest of the time. I look in the mirror at least once a day. I do not have a massive lunch on Sunday and starve for the rest of the week. I like my lunch every day! Very well, then, I should make a regular daily meal of my Bible reading. It can have an enormous impact on our lives if we come to it regularly, and allow it to affect the way we behave. It is life-transforming, no less.

I could cite any number of examples of the remarkable power this book has to change us for the better, but here is one from a particularly difficult part of the world, Cuba. The Cuban Bible Commission relate how they gave a Bible to a young prisoner called Armando. He was a complete rebel against society. His heart was full of bitterness. They were amazed that he accepted the Bible, but he did, and began to read it. 'With every visit,' they said, 'we saw his faith growing in leaps and bounds. Armando abandoned his bad behaviour and improved his attitude so much that he started to be known in the prison for his exemplary conduct. Today Armando is back outside, but now he is the one who takes his family to church. His former acquaintances are amazed at the dramatic new turn his life has taken.

'The only secret about this change lies in the Bible. It brought light into his prison cell and helped him transform his life to the point where he was leading other prisoners to God while still serving his sentence.'

Such is the transforming power of the word of God when we read and apply it regularly.

4

How can I begin?

If you were going out to a meal with a friend, you would certainly make some preparations: a wash and brush up, a comb through the hair, perhaps a change of clothes. Why should it be any different when we set out to meet with God?

Preparations

- *Get alone with God*   John Wesley, who was the key figure in the eighteenth-century Christian revival which probably saved England from revolution, used to get up to spend his daily time with God at 4.00 a.m. That puts me to shame. But I imagine he was able to get some privacy at that time of day! He wrote, 'I sit down alone . . . Only God is here. In his presence I open, I read his book. And what I read I teach.' Unless you get alone, it will be extremely hard to concentrate.

- *Get a regular time*   It is helpful to find a regular time of day when you can get apart with God. Our lives are so full that unless we build in a regular spot, we shall find that it simply does not happen. I know this is so – I have failed so often in this respect.

28

Many people find the morning the best time, before everything else crowds in.

- *Get a Bible you can enjoy* There is nothing to beat the King James version for beauty of language, but it is more than three hundred years old and not altogether easy to understand. So find one of the modern translations that you like. Either the New International Version or the Good News Bible would be an excellent choice.

- *Get right with God* Do you remember your mother calling you in to dinner, when you were a kid? 'Dinner's ready. Come and wash your hands!' That was wise advice, and it holds good for our time with God. We need to wash our hands first. We need to come to him and ask him to show us anything in our lives that has grieved him, confess it, and realise with deep gratitude that 'if we confess our sins, God is faithful and just and will forgive us our sins and purify us from all unrighteousness' (1 John 1:9).

- *Get 'on line'* You know how it is with your computer? You can type away on e-mail to your heart's content but it only communicates to anybody else when you get on line, and that requires a definite act on your part. Well, that has something to teach us. God's written word alone will not really communicate with us until we are 'on line' with God and ask him to make it come alive and speak to us through it. Before we start reading, we might find it helpful to use a short prayer, like the psalmist: 'Open my eyes that I may see wonderful things in your law' (Psalm 119:18).

The time together

Naturally the first thing to do is to read the passage you have chosen slowly a couple of times and see what strikes you. You will want to be clear on the main point of the passage, and then you will find it helpful to ask two questions.

Questions

First, 'What did this mean to the original recipients?' and second, 'If it meant that to them, what can it mean to me today?' If you don't ask the first question, you can read all sorts of things into scripture that were never intended by the writers. If you don't ask the second, you can find yourself in a desert of dry intellectual information that does nothing for your Christian life. Both questions are needed.

Some subsidiary questions are a great help in getting at the meat of the passage. I find it helpful to ask myself some such questions as these.

Is there something new about God that I can see in this passage?
Is there some example for me to follow?
Is there some warning for me to heed?
Is there a command to obey?
Is there a promise to claim?
Is there some fresh insight into the daily battle that I face?

What shall I take away as a Thought for the Day?

Reflection

As you go through those questions and apply them to what you have read, some of them will probably be irrelevant. There may be no warnings or promises in the passage you are looking at. But you are getting into the habit of asking questions of the text and letting it speak to you. That is the important thing. And some of those questions will certainly relate to what you have read. Let them be your gateways into the text. You may even like to use a small notebook to jot down what you have found helpful.

Prayer

Now is the time to reflect, meditate on what you have read, and to turn it into prayer and praise. Remember, you should be looking for a two-way conversation, and God most certainly is. He wants to hear from you in response to what he puts before you. Get into the way of praying over what you have read, *praying it in* to your heart and life.

Bible reading aids

In the next chapter we will explore how your time together with the Lord might be developed. But before I close this one I want to introduce you to one of the Bible reading aids which are readily available. The Scripture Union provide excellent notes at different levels. But I think I would suggest *New Daylight*, a popular series of daily Bible reading notes put out by the Bible Reading Fellowship. You can get them from

most good bookshops or from Sandy Lane West, Oxford, OX4 5HG. Each day a passage of scripture is printed, with helpful comment, followed by a prayer or a thought for the day. Here is a typical one, for you to sample. It is written by my wife!

1 Peter 2:9–12 God's people

But you are a chosen people, a royal priesthood, a holy nation, a people belonging to God, that you may declare the praises of him who called you out of darkness into his wonderful light. Once you were not a people, but now you are the people of God; once you had not received mercy, but now you have received mercy. Dear friends, I urge you, as aliens and strangers in the world, to abstain from sinful desires, which war against your soul. Live such good lives among the pagans that, though they accuse you of doing wrong, they may see your good deeds and glorify God on the day he visits us.

'But' . . . a small word for a major contrast. Peter's previous words had been of a person who disobeys Christ and finds him a stumbling-block. 'But you . . .' Peter is excited as he turns again to those who know Jesus as the foundation stone for life. Our faith in Jesus, though personal, is not individual. Every Christian who is linked with Jesus is joined with other Christians. 'You are a chosen people, a royal priesthood, a holy nation, a people belonging to God'. Each of those phrases shows tremendous privilege in the status we enjoy – chosen, royal, belonging to God – in our togetherness as his people.

But with privilege goes responsibility. We used to

be nobodies, outsiders, in darkness. Now we are special, insiders, in the light. So we want to show and tell others how wonderful he is. Not just by what we say, though our words are important if others are going to be able to understand what God has done for us and can do for them. But they will not want to listen to our words if our lives do not convey the same message. 'Live such good lives among the pagans' that however much they may want to complain about us, they cannot deny that God is real, alive and relevant in the late twentieth century as he was in the first.

And then the writer adds this conclusion:

> *To think about* 'Once you were . . .' 'Now you are . . .' How many things in your life are different because you belong to God's people?

As you can see, some notes like these, taking you through books of the Bible in short, easy-to-assimilate passages, have a lot to be said for them. But let me give you a warning. Don't read the notes until you have got 'on line' with God yourself and seen what you can find in the passage. Otherwise it can all be rather second hand, and that is a disaster in any relationship!

5

How can I get the best out of it?

I promised in the last chapter that you and I would dig into a passage of scripture together, and see what we could find. Right, let's go for it. Suppose we are due to look at Psalm 27, in the course of our reading.

The alarm goes off, and because we have placed it quite deliberately out of reach, we almost *have* to get up to turn the wretched thing off. Cold water works wonders on sleepy faces, and before long we are dressed, more or less in our right mind, and with a cup of coffee in our hand. We see that Psalm 27 beckons. We put the coffee down, and reverently ask the Lord to cleanse us from anything we have failed to confess to him, so that there is no blockage in our time together. And then we ask him to shine his light on the page, so that it leaps to life for us. OK? Then we'll read the psalm.

1   The Lord is my light and my salvation – whom shall I fear? The Lord is the stronghold of my life – of whom shall I be afraid?

2   When evil men advance against me to devour my flesh, when my enemies and my foes attack me, they will stumble and fall.

3   Though an army besiege me, my heart will not fear; though war break out against me, even then will I be confident.

4   One thing I ask of the Lord, this is what I seek; that I may dwell in the house of the Lord all the days of my life, to gaze upon the beauty of the Lord and to seek him in his temple.

5   For in the day of trouble he will keep me safe in his dwelling; he will hide me in the shelter of his tabernacle and set me high upon a rock.

6   Then my head will be exalted above the enemies who surround me; at his tabernacle will I sacrifice with shouts of joy. I will sing and make music to the Lord.

7   Hear my voice when I call, O Lord; be merciful to me and answer me.

8   To you, O my heart, he has said, 'Seek my face.' Your face, Lord, I will seek.

9   Do not hide your face from me, do not turn your servant away in anger; you have been my helper. Do not reject me or forsake me, O God my Saviour.

10   Though my father and mother forsake me, the Lord will receive me.

11   Teach me your way, O Lord; lead me in a straight path because of my oppressors.

12   Do not hand me over to the desire of my foes, for false witnesses rise up against me, breathing out violence.

13   I am still confident of this: I will see the

goodness of the Lord in the land of the living.
14   Wait for the Lord; be strong and take heart and wait for the Lord.

Let's read it over again, slowly. It is not difficult to see what the psalm is about. It is written by King David, in the midst of the many troubles of his reign, and it expresses his deep confidence in the Lord, come what may. That's not a bad tip for my life, as well. So I'll turn it into a prayer:

Lord, please give me that deep underlying confidence in you which David had.

Now, let's see how the psalm is made up. The first three verses reflect on the Lord's reliability, the second three on David's resolve, and then it moves into prayer from verses 7 to 12, ending with a final expression of confidence in the Lord. Reflection, prayer, confidence. A good pattern for me to pick up from time to time. I think I'll jot that down in my little notebook for today.

Is there, I wonder, *something new about God* that I can see in this passage? Why, yes. I don't need to go beyond the first verse. I can imagine David rejoicing in God as his light in the dark and his saviour in tough times. But those things are not only true for David! The Lord is *my* light, not just other people's. Light, that's worth pondering on. It is light that makes things grow. It is light that brings joy after a dark night. Light shows us the way, and is a beacon in the gloom. My, there's a lot in this concept of light! And it all comes from God. He is the true light, but he is also *my* light. I know him and trust him – I have this

personal relationship with him. That is wonderful. May I never take it for granted.

He is my salvation, too. Not quite sure what that means but it is clearly all to do with rescue and wholeness. I am glad God is my salvation. I'm going to tell him so.

Lord, it is wonderful to think of you as my light and my salvation. Thank you with all my heart.

Right, is there some *example* for me to follow? There are several, I think. David's attitude in this psalm has a lot to teach me. But I am amazed in particular by verse 8. It seems that David is becoming aware that God wants him to 'seek his face'. And David's glad and eager response is, 'Your face, Lord, I will seek.' It is simply astonishing that the Lord of heaven and earth should invite human beings into his company, and should actually *want* to have us in touch with him. But it is no less astonishing how slow we are – or at any rate I am – to take advantage of this gracious offer. After all, if I had an invitation from the Queen of England saying, in effect, 'Seek my face,' I would jump at it with enthusiasm. Why then am I so reluctant to get out of bed in the morning to meet the King of kings? I have a lot to learn from David's response.

Lord, I don't think I had quite realised the enormous privilege it is to have an audience with you. I hadn't seen you were longing to meet me. May this go deep into my heart, and motivate me to get out of bed to meet you, especially when I am reluctant to do so on these cold mornings.

Is there some *warning* to heed? I don't think there is. So what else should I look for? Ah yes, is there some *fresh insight* into the daily battle we face? Well, there seems to be a lot in the psalm about that. There are several references to the enemies and dangers besetting King David. Let's see. Yes, he speaks of 'evil men', 'enemies and foes' (a whole 'army' of them), 'trouble', 'rejection', 'oppressors' and 'false witnesses'. I need not kid myself that it was easier for them to lead a godly life in those far off days! I certainly don't have an army coming to attack me, but I have my enemies all right. I have the false witnesses who spread untrue gossip about me at work. I know both trouble and rejection. So can I learn anything from David's reactions? Well, verse 2 suggests that enemies are to be expected. I should not be surprised when this happens to me. Second, he seems to have conquered the fear factor (verse 3). His confidence really is in the Lord. Third, he describes God's protection in a marvellous way. It is as if he hides us deep in a safe cave, or puts us on top of some great rock where the waves cannot reach us. Lovely pictures those – worth thinking about.

Lord, I so easily panic when trouble comes or when I get slandered. Please help me not to be surprised by this sort of thing, and to experience the confidence you can give in place of fear. And please keep me safe through the pressures that I realise are bound to come. Because, Lord, I do want to be a credit to you.

What about a *promise*? Is there one here? Oh yes, verse 10. 'Though my father and mother forsake me, the Lord will receive me.' Wow! That really is something. My parents would give the shirt off their backs for me, but even if they were to disown me, the Lord will receive me. That's amazing generosity.

Lord, I find that promise overwhelming. Thank you so much.

Is there, I wonder, a *prayer* that I could make my own? Yes, we've scored again. Verse 11 is superb. 'Teach me your way, O Lord.' All too often I pray, 'Bless the way I have chosen, O Lord.' But this is much better. The Lord knows what is best for my life. I need to ask him to have his will with me, not to bless my will!

Lord, keep me praying that your will be done in my life, not mine.

It's time for breakfast and then off to work. But is there something I want to take away and chew over at odd moments in the day? Maybe it could be verse 4. King David clearly longed to spend time in the 'house of the Lord' for the twin purposes of simply gazing on his beauty and bringing requests to him. I don't need to go into a building for that (though it might be no bad idea to nip into that church nearby for five minutes at lunchtime). But I do want to keep close to the Lord, so that I can enjoy his presence and bring needs to him at any time. No, good as that is, it is all too much of a mouthful to take away as a *thought for the day*. I can't do better than the final verse: 'Wait for the Lord.' I am so impetuous, so reluctant to wait. But time and again I have discovered that although the good Lord often runs it fine he is never late. I'm going to wait for you today!

> *Lord, that has been a really helpful time with you this morning. May it show in how I behave today. Please keep me looking to you for courage if the going gets rough today. Thanks so much that you are my light and my salvation. I really do want to keep close to you so that I can simply enjoy your beauty and bring my requests to you. And Lord, please guide me today – and I really do want your way, not mine.*

No, I know this is not very sophisticated Bible study. But it is the response of an amateur, a lover, to the Lord who says to us, 'Seek my face!' It's no bad way to get started.

6

How can I avoid getting stale?

One of the dangers in Bible reading is boredom. If you do the same thing in the same way day after day in any walk of life, you run the risk of getting bored. Why should it be any different with reading the Bible? The approach we looked at in the last couple of chapters is a valuable servant if you want to get regular spiritual food from the Bible, but it is a bad master if it leads to boredom.

Variety is what is needed. There are more ways than one to read the Bible profitably. In this chapter we shall examine two of them.

Read a whole book

Naturally you will not have leisure to do that very often, but occasionally it can be very refreshing. After all, the books of the Bible were not designed to be read in ten-verse portions! You gain an overview of the purpose of the book as a whole when you give yourself time to read it through at a sitting.

Maybe begin with a very short letter, like Philemon, which would have been written on just one page of papyrus. Ask yourself who wrote it, to whom and why. Those are good questions. In this case it is clear who wrote it, the apostle Paul. He wrote it to one of his own converts, Philemon, and the house church he led. Philemon appears to have been a landowner whose slave, Onesimus, had stolen money, run away and been imprisoned. His companion in prison was none other than the apostle Paul, who found himself incarcerated for his faith. Well, Paul led this runaway slave to Christ. Now he is writing to ask Philemon to forgive Onesimus and have him back, once he is released from prison. This would have been an unheard-of thing in the ancient world: runaway slaves were crucified if caught! Moreover, Paul wants Philemon not just to have Onesimus back as a slave but to welcome him as a beloved Christian brother. What an astonishing little letter! It spells social revolution and the end of distinctions between slave and free. Just think what dynamics are released when both master and slave are brought to Christ. There is great power to change society in this book you are reading!

I have just come across a remarkable example of this. Dr Mae Alice Reggy, currently a Bible Society consultant, tells of a practice among the villagers of north Ghana. When a family was deep in debt they would often settle it by giving one of their daughters as a slave to the *juju* or fetish priest. These girls were regularly abused and raped. When the Christian workers first arrived they taught these girls literacy and then gave them Bibles in their own Éwé dialect. This resulted in many conversions: the girls came to see how much God valued them. They began to escape from the fetish priests, who resorted to their traditional magic in order to restrain them. It did not work on Christian girls! Soon more girls began to leave. This attracted attention from the media. The girls said on camera, 'We have learned to read and we have read about Jesus. Now we are Christians and we are leaving this old way of life for a new one.' The fetish priests, of course, accused the girls of rebelling against their culture. A lively debate ensued. But the outcome was that the government abolished the practice, returned the girls to their homes, and outlawed human bondage as a way of settling debts. Today, as in the first century, whole communities can be changed by the power of God's word.

Liberation, then, is clearly the main point of this little letter to Philemon. But as you read it over again you cannot help being struck by a number of other things: the great courtesy and tact of the apostle, his refusal to lay down the law to Philemon (instead he appealed to his better nature), the emphasis on hospitality, the importance of the church in the home, the humour, the love, the passion for evangelism even in prison – and a lot more. You could have a fascinating time of discovery as you range over the twenty-five verses of this short letter.

Or think of a rather longer letter in the New Testament, the first letter of Peter. It is full of profound material, so we tend to read it in very small bits. But it is great to read at a sitting and see its very clear overview. Peter wrote it to Christians scattered around the eastern Mediterranean to encourage them at a time when they were suffering a good deal of unpopularity

because of their stand as Christians. It led to fierce opposition and harassment from their colleagues at work. If you are facing ostracism or even harassment in your work or social life because you are a Christian, it might be invaluable to stand back from the situation a little and see it through the lens of this letter, written to provide encouragement to Christians long ago in a similar situation.

Or suppose you feel overwhelmed at the sheer nastiness of modern life, with its human corruption, unceasing wars, famines, disasters and the nuclear threat. Why not take a leisurely read in the book of Revelation? You won't understand it all, any more than you 'understand' an intricate sonata or a complicated painting, but let the main point of it grab you. The main point is very obvious. St John is writing to Christian communities in various key cities which are going through apocalyptic times under a totalitarian regime, and he wants to show them the true realities of the situation. He wants to take them behind the scenes into God's control room, so to speak, and help them to realise that the Lord God omnipotent really is reigning, despite appearances. In the graphic wording of the book of Revelation, 'the Lamb who was slain is in the midst of the throne of God'. So ultimate victory is assured. It is God, not pain, death and disaster, who will have the last word. No wonder this book has been so prized by persecuted Christians the world over.

Or maybe you are just feeling fed up. You have been a Christian for some time, and you are reluctant to get involved in some area of service to God which you know perfectly well you should do. Right, read the book of Jonah at a sitting. He felt just like that. He intended to travel as far away as he could from God's purpose for his life, and God went to extraordinary lengths to bring him back on track. Once he returned to the path of obedience he found how happy and fulfilling it was. Highly relevant stuff, is it not?

The book of Judges speaks very directly to our postmodern society, where we all want to 'do our own thing'. It tells us about a society where everyone 'did what was right in their own eyes'. The result was chaotic, and God's people were overwhelmed by a variety of enemies and disasters. But in successive generations, when they cried to the Lord for help and really meant it, he answered them and raised up leader after leader to deliver them.

Yes, to read a whole book, long or short, at a sitting is a very useful variation in Bible reading. Here is another.

Immerse yourself in a single verse

Just as in mining you sometimes strike a particularly rich vein, so in Bible reading you sometimes come across such a profound verse that it merits your full attention for the time you have at your disposal. For example, 1 Peter 3:18 is all about what the death of Jesus means for us, and it is very deep. This is what it says.

> For Christ died for sins once for all, the righteous for the unrighteous, to bring you to God.

Just think about that for a moment. Concentrate on

each word or phrase. In the previous verses, Peter has been talking about innocent suffering, and that leads him on to the supreme example of innocent suffering, where the best person who ever lived died the most cruel death ever invented.

Who was this awesome sufferer? Why it was the *Christ*, God's anointed one, the climax of God's revelation, the one who had been so longingly awaited by prophets and men of faith down the centuries.

Was it easy for him to go to the cross? Not at all. It involved the most excruciating suffering and culminated in *death*. Death by crucifixion was the most ghastly form of torment known to man.

Why, then, did he do it? He went to the cross not because he wanted to make some grand heroic gesture, not because the Mafia caught up with him, not to show how much God loved us (how could torturing his Son show that?). No, he went there *for sins*, not his own but the sins of the whole world.

Well, you say, 'I still don't understand that sort of talk. What does it mean?' It means, says Peter, that he, the *righteous* one, stood in for us, the *unrighteous* ones. I can't quarrel with that description either of him or of us, can you? It was '*the righteous for the unrighteous*'. It must mean, then, that Christ voluntarily underwent our doom, carried our burden, expunged our guilt – and it cost him Calvary to do it. Amazing grace indeed!

'But that was a long time ago. Does something of the sort not need repeating?' It does not. His death for the rescue of mankind was '*once for all*'. It never needs repeating. However many human beings there have ever been or ever will be, their number is still finite. The self-sacrifice of the God–man Jesus Christ was infinite. It availed for Abraham centuries before Christ was born. It avails for you and me, centuries after.

But it is not automatic in its operation. The whole purpose of the cross, Peter tells us, was *'to bring you to God'*. God was alienated by all the evil in my life and yours. At Calvary that alienation was abolished for those who allow Jesus to bring them to his heavenly Father. The purpose of the at-one-ment (which is what the technical term 'atonement' means) is achieved when we let Christ cleanse us and bring us to the Father's presence – 'ransomed, healed, restored, forgiven' as the hymn writer put it. What a lot there is in that single verse.

Now apply that method of digging deep into the text to something like St Paul's great motto:

I want to know Christ and the power of his resurrection and the fellowship of sharing in his sufferings, becoming like him in his death, and so, somehow, to attain to the resurrection from the dead. (Philippians 3:10–11)

Notice the supreme aim of this old Christian warrior, *'to know Christ'*. That is what Christianity is all about. 'But,' we might ask him, 'did you not get to know Christ years ago on the Damascus Road?' 'Indeed I did,' he would reply. 'But that was only the beginning of our relationship, the introductions, so to speak. I want to go on to know him more and more.' And if we press him on what that would involve, he has a clear answer for us. It will mean *'the power of his resurrection'*. He wants to see God releasing in our frail mortal lives the very same power which raised Christ from the grave! Reflect on the moral transformation and spiritual dynamism which that suggests.

But there is nothing triumphalist about Christianity. We are bound to experience suffering as well as victory. And Paul knows that *'the fellowship of sharing in his sufferings'*, in hardships, rejection and illness, is a great way to deepen that intimacy with Christ which the apostle craved. There must, in fact, be a conscious and daily dying to the old life and a rising to the new life if we are to develop healthy Christian lives. We will have to *'become like him in his death'*. Paul has more to say on the subject, you may have discovered, in 2 Corinthians 4:10. And somehow it will all end with our sharing in *'the resurrection from the dead'* which Jesus pioneered. A magnificent and profound goal for any Christian to pursue.

What we have done in this chapter is to take a telescope and a magnifying glass to our Bible study. The first has given us an overview of what we are reading; the second has enabled us to look at it in detail. Both are valuable ways to avoid getting stuck in a rut. There are other methods, and we shall turn to them next.

7

How can I go deeper?

Do you want to take your Bible reading to a deeper level? Well, you don't need to go to theological college or anything like that, but there are three basic tools that will be an enormous help to you.

Acquire the tools

The first is a *concordance*. That is a book where you can look up any word that comes in the Bible and find its reference. If you looked up 'joy', for example, it would give you all the places where the word occurs in the Bible. I think it was Alexander Cruden, who lived nearly three hundred years ago, who first compiled this valuable book. It was an amazing achievement to record each occurrence of every word in the King James version of the Bible, without the aid of a computer. On top of that, he suffered throughout his life from very bad health. We owe Mr Cruden a great debt of gratitude. I personally am particularly thankful for his book (which has an honoured place on my shelves), because I often half-remember snatches of the Bible in the King James version, on which I was brought up, and want to track them down.

But, of course, the Cruden Concordance will be no use to you if you are using one of the modern translations of the Bible. So go to your bookseller and ask for the appropriate concordance for your preferred version. They have these things on disk, too. All of which means it should be easy to trace any reference you want to follow up in the Bible. We shall see below how useful this is.

A second very valuable Bible reading aid is a *commentary*. This tells you the authorship, background and circumstances of each of the Bible books, and offers a commentary on it, which can be very illuminating, especially with some of the difficult bits.

The third book you will find useful is a *Bible dictionary*. This gives you detailed information about any subject mentioned in the Bible. There would be pages on 'Egypt', for example, telling you about the history and customs of Egypt, since that country is often mentioned in the Bible. If you looked up 'book', it would tell you about the origins of writing, how the early books were made, and so on. Suppose you wonder what a difficult Bible word like 'justification' really means, or what is known of an obscure person like Demas, your Bible dictionary will help you out. We are much indebted to the Inter-Varsity Press for publishing both these valuable Bible aids, and keeping them constantly up to date. They are the *New Bible Commentary* and the *New Bible Dictionary*. They have been compiled by good scholars, have an enormous international circulation and you can rely on them. Reference books like these are not cheap, but that is what Christmas and birthdays are for! Drop the hint in the right place and the books may well materialise.

If not, they are worth saving up for. You will not regret buying them.

Right, then. We have the equipment. How shall we proceed?

Study a character

Biographies are always fascinating, and the Bible is full of them. It does not tell us all we would like to know about the characters it portrays, but it certainly offers us clear examples and warnings from their lives. 'For everything that was written in the past was written to teach us, so that through endurance and the encouragement of the Scriptures we might have hope' (Romans 15:4). The Old Testament books of Chronicles seem to be specially written to teach important lessons to future generations through the lives they record. Many of these concern the kings of Israel and Judah. It is well worth first looking at the background to each story (that is where your commentary and dictionary may help), then at the steps God took to prepare the man for his life's work, then at how God used him, followed by the aftermath – did his later years show spiritual growth or decline? Each of these people leaves us with some overall lesson to apply to our own lives.

Let us take an example from the New Testament. Had you noticed how most of the twelve apostles never seem to do anything as individuals? They are just 'the Twelve', and all we know about them is their names. Well, Andrew is no exception. He is just one in the list of names – except in St John's Gospel. Here he appears three times, and he is always introducing someone else to Jesus.

In chapter 1 he brings his brother Simon Peter to Jesus (v. 41). That was a pretty significant move!

In chapter 6 we read of thousands of very hungry people hanging on Jesus' words. But how could they get anything to eat in the back of beyond where there were no shops? It is Andrew who stumbles on the answer. He gets chatting to a boy who has a lunch bag of five barley cakes and two little fish. He introduces him to Jesus (6:8). The boy is willing to hand over his lunch, and Jesus miraculously transforms it into food for the whole multitude. We know the story well. It is recorded in all four Gospels, and is as certain as anything Jesus did. But we often forget Andrew. If he had not introduced the lad to Jesus, the miracle would never have taken place.

The third occasion where Andrew appears is in chapter 12 when some Greeks, who had come up to the Passover festival, were so keen to meet Jesus. It was Andrew and his brother Philip, both of them with Greek names, who got alongside these Greeks and introduced them to Jesus (v. 22).

So we have only three little cameos of this man, but each of them shows him doing the same thing. We are never told that he preached a sermon, but he clearly had a passion for bringing people into touch with Jesus. First, someone in his own family. Then someone whom most people would not have bothered about. Then folk who were outside the religious circles of the day. What an example for us!

Or think of Abraham, to whom Jews, Muslims and Christians all look back for inspiration. He was the first stirring example of how God deals with mankind and what he expects from us. God comes to Abraham in *sheer love*, and offers to make him the father of many nations (Genesis 12:2; 15:5). The response he looks for is *sheer faith* in Abraham – and indeed in us. His faith is the main thing for which Abraham is remembered in the Bible. The Genesis account shows us four significant aspects of it.

First, Abraham *responded to God's call* (15:6). He entered into a personal trusting relationship with God. That is where true faith begins.

Second, Abraham *obeyed God's command* (12:1, 4). He left his country for an unknown destination, in trusting obedience to the God who had called him. Apart from one or two lapses that obedience marked all his subsequent life.

Third, Abraham *looked to God's future* (12:7; 17:3–8). He had no possessions whatsoever in the land of Canaan, and yet God had promised it to him. He had no children, and yet God had promised he would be the father of many nations. God's promises proved to be a beacon of hope in the darkness.

Fourth, Abraham *trusted God's faithfulness* (15:6). He 'believed the Lord' and God 'credited it to him as righteousness'. That faith was tested through and through. Tested by having no stake at all in Canaan although the land had been promised to him. Tested by having no children until well after he was too old. Tested by allowing Lot to choose the best land, and relying on God to fulfil what he had undertaken.

Authentic faith is still marked by all four of those characteristics.

Now that is only skimming the surface of what

Abraham's faith was, and what ours could be. But it gives enough of a foretaste, perhaps, to drive us into a fuller and more detailed study of this amazing man's life.

I wonder if you are intrigued by detective stories? The Bible offers you plenty of scope to do your own detective work. St Luke is a good example. He was the author both of his Gospel and of the Acts, though he declines to attach his name to either. Clearly he was a self-effacing man. If we look him up in our concordance, what can we discover? Only three references. In his letter to the Colossians, Paul refers to 'our dear friend Luke, the doctor' (4:14). The apostle had clearly benefited from the medical knowledge of this dear friend who was prepared willingly to enter prison with him. In Philemon 24 he is referred to as a 'fellow-worker'. So his work for the gospel was not confined to his medical skill. And in 2 Timothy 4:11 we get a glimpse of his loyalty to Paul and the extent to which the apostle valued him, in the pathetic note: 'Only Luke is with me.' Luke had accompanied Paul to his last imprisonment in Rome from where that final letter was written.

That is all we can tell on the surface. But let us read between the lines. There are three places in his account in the Acts where Luke slips from talking about 'they' to 'we'. He is quietly informing us that he was there. The first place is in Acts 16:10–17. Luke turns up in Troas and accompanies Paul and his entourage to Philippi where they conduct the first ever mission in Europe. This results in a small company of new believers and the inference is that Luke stays with them, since the narrative then returns to 'they'. Several

years later we find that the next 'we' passage begins where the last one had left off, in Philippi (20:5–21). It is not difficult to guess what Luke had been doing in those intervening years. He had been building up that little church at Philippi. It had grown to have its own 'overseers and deacons' (Philippians 1:1) and Paul's letter shows how far their Christian lives had progressed. If you had built up a church from almost nothing to that level, would you not have mentioned it? I'm afraid I would. But not Luke!

The third 'we' passage is no less illuminating. It stretches from Acts 27:1 to 28:16. We had left Luke in Palestine at the end of the last 'we' section (21:17), and almost immediately Paul was practically lynched by the mob and spent two years in prison in Caesarea before he appealed to the emperor and was sent to Rome for trial. What was Luke doing in those two years? Surely he was gathering information for his Gospel. He tells us that he had researched it carefully (Luke 1:3). He would have had access to many of the main actors in the story of Jesus, including the Virgin Mary. She is, doubtless, the source of his accounts of Jesus' birth and childhood. And although Luke keeps himself rigorously out of the Gospel, we can discover a little about him from the events he decides to include. He chooses incidents which highlight women, Samaritans and Gentiles – outsiders, all of them. He underlines Jesus' love for the poor, and his warnings against the seductions of wealth. He has much to say about the power of the Holy Spirit and of prayer in both of his volumes. These must surely represent some of the concerns of Luke himself, and enable us to see what sort of a man he was.

Finally, in his last 'we' passage he gives us a vivid account of that terrible sea journey, the shipwreck and the final arrival in Rome. There he leaves Paul in his own hired house, arguing the Christian case with all who came to see him – bound in body but free in spirit.

All of this is fair inference from what the text actually tells us, and it makes a fascinating study. The Bible affords us plenty of others.

Examine a chapter

Instead of reading a few verses it is sometimes useful to examine a whole chapter. Take Romans 8, for example. In this marvellous chapter we find Paul laying before us the whole spread of salvation, past, present and future.

In verses 1–4 he dares to make the claim that 'Therefore, there is now no condemnation for those who are in Christ Jesus' because his atoning death on the cross has cleared our debts and enables us to stand tall before God, knowing that our accusing past will never again be dragged up to shame us.

In the middle of that chapter he concentrates on the present. Paul is not blind to our pains and adversities, but he remains confident because of the presence of the Holy Spirit in each Christian life. It is the Spirit who assures us we belong to God's family (v. 16), enables us to know him as Father (indeed, 'Daddy' is what the Aramaic word *Abba* really means, v. 15), sets us free progressively from the downward pull of sin (v. 2), helps us to pray (v. 26) and cooperates with us in everything for our good (v. 28).

Consequently we can have every confidence as we face the future. God's plan is that we may be made like Jesus and live with him for ever (vv. 29, 30). So 'If God is for us, who can be against us?' (v. 31) 'Who shall separate us from the love of Christ? Shall trouble or hardship or persecution or famine or nakedness or danger or sword? ... No, in all these things we are more than conquerors through him who loved us' (vv. 35–7). Paul ends with a purple passage of confident faith and hope, 'For I am convinced that neither death nor life ... neither the present nor the future ... nor anything else in all creation, will be able to separate us from the love of God that is in Christ Jesus our Lord' (vv. 38–9). What a chapter!

But you may feel this is special pleading. Not all chapters yield the riches of Romans 8. True, but there are treasures to be found in lots of them. Take 2 Timothy 2, for instance. Here we see seven pen pictures of the Christian worker. Paul points to the faithfulness of the steward (a responsible official in a great house who looks after the other servants, v. 2), the endurance of the soldier (v. 3), the self-discipline of the athlete (v. 5), the hard work of the farmer (v. 6), the craftsman's skill with his tools (v. 15), the cleanliness of tableware (v. 20) and the wholeheartedness of the servant or slave (v. 24). We all need those characteristics, and the broad overview of a chapter can sometimes prove particularly instructive.

Follow up a theme or a word

There are many great themes which run through the Bible: God's covenant mercies to his people, the faithful remnant in the midst of a fallen world, the kingdom of God, the justification of sinners, God's purposes for community life and so forth. Important topics like family life, punishment and forgiveness, sexual behaviour, marriage and singleness, work and money are all given extensive treatment in the Bible. It is instructive to gather up the teaching about them that you find in different parts of scripture. Your concordance will be a real ally, and you might even invest in a topical concordance, which deals not with individual words but with subjects treated in the Bible.

So follow a theme, but you will often find it is easier and just as fruitful to concentrate on a single significant word or phrase. I remember being much helped by a study I once did on 'the will of God'. I found the scriptures have quite a lot to say on the subject. I did another on our 'calling' and our 'inheritance' and found it inspiring. 'Take heed' was another one (based on the King James version). I must *take heed* what sort of life I build on the only true foundation, Jesus himself (1 Corinthians 3:10). I need to *take heed* lest I fall, especially when I am feeling confident (1 Corinthians 10:12). I must *take heed* how I exercise my Christian liberty, in case it brings me into a new bondage (1 Corinthians 8:9) and must *take heed* to 'complete the work' I have received from the Lord (Colossians 4:17). Daily I must *take heed* to let the light of scripture dawn on my path (2 Peter 1:19). Not only is that a

comprehensive study for myself. I shall have something by me to share with others if the opportunity
arises.

I want to end this chapter by looking at the single
word *able* and showing how its various occurrences
can speak directly to the things people sometimes say.

- *I really am a can of worms. If only they knew what I am
  like inside* Hebrews 7:25 speaks decisively to that
  fear. 'He is *able* to save completely those who come
  to God through him, because he always lives to
  intercede for them.'
- *I think I am a committed Christian, but I really am not
  sure he has accepted me* Here, 2 Timothy 1:12 is very
  helpful. 'I am not ashamed, because I know whom I
  have believed and am convinced that he is *able* to
  guard what I have entrusted to him.'
- *I am not convinced that prayer does any
  good* Ephesians 3:20 replies, 'Now to him who is
  able to do immeasurably more than all we ask or
  imagine, according to his power that is at work
  within us, to him be glory in the church and in
  Christ Jesus throughout all generations.'
- *I'm so critical of other people* But as Romans 14:4
  reminds us, 'Who are you to judge someone else's
  servant? To his own master he stands or falls. And
  he will stand, for the Lord is *able* to make him stand.'
- *I'm afraid to give as I should. I need financial
  security* 'Remember this: Whoever sows sparingly
  will also reap sparingly, and whoever gives generously will also reap generously. Each man should
  give what he has decided in his heart to give, not
  reluctantly or under compulsion, for God loves a

cheerful giver. And God is *able* to make all grace abound to you, so that in all things at all times, having all that you need, you will abound in every good work' (2 Corinthians 9:6–8).

- *My temptations overwhelm me. There seems no way out* But in Hebrews 2:18 we read, 'Because he himself suffered when he was tempted, he is *able* to help those who are being tempted.'
- *This Christian life is so difficult. Will I ever make good*? 'To him who is *able* to keep you from falling and to present you before his glorious presence without fault and with great joy . . . be glory . . . for evermore' (Jude 24).

Do you feel you could never have worked that out? Yes you could! All I did was to take my concordance, see the references to 'able' and apply them to the real world I have to live in. You can do the same. That is what the Bible is for.

8

Why not read it with a friend?

So far we have been thinking of Bible reading on our own. In the next two chapters I want to say something about reading it with others. First, let's see how a couple of friends can encourage one another enormously by reading some scripture together on a regular basis.

The importance of personal nurture

When someone has come to a clear decision to follow Christ they very much need this sort of help. I vividly recall the early days of my own discipleship. I used to meet up once a week for half an hour or so with Richard Gorrie, who had helped me to faith. He would suggest a passage of scripture for us to read together. We would do so, turn some of our insights into prayer, and then I was free to raise any of the problems in my early Christian life that I wanted to share with him. To have an older Christian at hand like this was invaluable. It was a great way for me to learn to grow.

There is a real need for this sort of thing throughout the Christian community. Sadly, in many churches little attempt is made to introduce anyone at all to Christ: the church seems to be a club for insiders. Where there is a definite effort to win people to Christ, the follow-up is frequently very weak. The new believer is expected to sink or swim in this new church environment, which may be quite alien to him. Singing hymns, seeing a clergyman in operation, listening to prayers being read, listening to sermons which make assumptions he does not share – all this may be quite outside his experience. It is ironical that the Church of England, which revised its services in order to make them more intelligible, should start its main service, the Communion, on page 119 of a substantial book! Not much help for the amateur there. Clearly the new Christian needs some gentle tuition in the new life on which he has embarked.

Mercifully, the Alpha Course is proving invaluable as an introduction to discipleship, but that is a group affair and does not provide the intimacy of the one-to-one session. You only have to ask yourself whether you gain more from being part of a computer class when you are learning, or whether you do better with someone sitting alongside you. I know what helps me most.

Because of this lack of personal nurturing, a great many converts to the faith never get the grounding they need. People hope they will get stuck in and grow, and some do. But many fall by the wayside, because no disciplined effort has been made to mentor them. One of the greatest things we can do for a new believer is to have a number of sessions with him or her, reading carefully chosen passages of the Bible together, praying things over, and allowing any of the problems that are inevitable in the early stages of discipleship to surface. I dread to think where I would be now if Richard had not taken that trouble with me.

Right, how shall we go about it? Let us suppose that your friend Bill has come to the point in his life when he is ready to entrust his life to Christ, and that you are the one who has been the last link in the chain bringing him to that point. Very well, it is your responsibility to help him to get his sea legs on the ship of faith. He is going to need help, particularly if, like most people these days, he has had no Christian background. Other people will doubtless teach him a lot, but he will have a special bond with you because you led him to the Lord. St Paul was well aware of the power of that link. He wrote to the Corinthians, 'Even though you have ten thousand guardians in Christ, you do not have many fathers, for in Christ Jesus I became your father through the gospel' (1 Corinthians 4:15). Your relationship with him as a 'father' will be unique. You must make good use of it. For he will take advice and guidance from you that he might spurn from anyone else.

The time together

You will naturally suggest to your friend Bill that you get together soon after he has fumbled his way to some sort of commitment. That is one of the most critical times of all, when doubts fester, he is not sure what he has done, and the pull of the old life is strong.

So meet him soon. Have a Bible for yourself and bring one along for him too, in case he has not got one.

The first session

In this first time together you will want one thing to become crystal clear – that this act of commitment to Christ is no bizarre oddity, as he may be feeling, but an essential for all Christians. So choose a passage which illustrates that act of surrender and new life. Three good ones are the story of Zacchaeus (Luke 19:1–10), the story of Nicodemus (John 3:1–18) and the story of the conversion of Saul of Tarsus (Acts 9:1–25). Suppose we choose the third of these.

You will each turn to the passage, pray for insight and read it through. Make sure he reads at least half the passage, so as to get used to the sound of his own voice reading the Bible! Then suggest a couple of minutes of complete silence as each of you looks for some helpful thought that can be shared with the other. It would be wise for you to give the lead after those two minutes are over: 'I loved verse 8 and the way Saul changed from being a macho leader anxious to beat up the Christians in Damascus, to allowing others to lead him into the place – once God had started changing him. I wonder if you have noticed any changes yet in your own experience?' He will say if he has noticed anything of the kind yet, and you might then ask him, 'What bit did you like most, as you read it through – and why?' Always ensure that you are both trying to see what it meant in the original situation, and then how that can apply to your own lives. As we saw in an earlier chapter, both are necessary.

What you want him to see from this first session is that God can change the life of the most determined opponent: conversion is perfectly natural and very common. You want him to see also that though we may not go through the same psychological sequences as Saul, and though our coming to faith may be much less spectacular and more gradual than his, four elements in Saul's conversion hold good for everyone. First, Saul came to recognise he was in the wrong persecuting Christians (v. 4). Second, he came to recognise Jesus as the Lord of glory (v. 5). Third, he made an act of surrender to him (vv. 6–9). And fourth, his subsequent life showed the difference. Some of those differences seem to have been almost immediate. He began to tell others (v. 20). He grew spiritually (v. 22). He abandoned his old behaviour pattern (v. 21). He accepted ministry from Ananias, whom only a few days earlier he would have thrown into prison. He discovered Christian fellowship with Ananias, his 'brother' (v. 17). He was baptised and filled with the Holy Spirit (v. 18) and he tasted the first signs of opposition from those who used to be his colleagues (v. 23).

These are some of the truths that you will want to see your friend discover. It does not matter if you do not discuss them all. It matters enormously that he begins to find the Bible is a book that speaks to him, begins to pick verses and apply them to his life, and begins to talk to you without embarrassment about spiritual things. You may want to prompt him, by directing his attention to a particular verse so that he discovers its truths for himself. Could he say, like Saul, that he has begun to see who Jesus really is? Has his conscience, like Saul's, been pricked into repentance? Has he fallen at the feet of Jesus in surrender? Has he begun to notice any difference in his life? Is he aware of the Holy Spirit's presence inside him? You might even turn to Romans 8:15, where he can see that the first job of the Spirit when he takes up residence in the believer is to assure him he belongs in God's family.

By a judicious mixture of contributing some of these thoughts yourself and asking him what he reckons a particular verse means, you will cover most of the main points in this stirring passage, and he will be able to see that there is nothing odd about the surrender to Christ he has made. He is simply following the greatest of the apostles.

You will then probably want to suggest a short time of prayer. To get him started, suggest that neither of you uses more than one sentence, that you speak in your own natural words (not attempting any high-flown 'religious' jargon) and that you turn a thought that each of you has found helpful while reading the Bible into a one-sentence prayer or thank-you. Start off yourself, so that you can model it a bit for him. 'Verse 15. Thank you, Lord, so much, that you have called Bill, like Saul long ago, to be a chosen instrument for you to carry your name before others, Amen' or 'Verse 10. "The Lord called to Ananias." Lord, make both of us really sensitive to your voice when you want us to do something for you, just as Ananias was.'

He will soon break the sound barrier, and follow your example in prayer. If he bursts out, 'I can't pray!' you might gently respond, 'Yes, you can. You can talk to me: so you can talk to the Lord. He has promised to be among us when two or three gather in his name. Tell him what is on your heart.' And in my experience that almost always liberates the 'Bills' of this world to start praying aloud, which is something they are going to find valuable during their Christian lives.

That is quite enough input for your first session. There needs to be time for relaxed conversation, and for him to bring up anything that is troubling him. It has been an important 'first': the first time he has read a passage of the Bible in this way; the first time he has done so with another person; the first time he has commented on it aloud and prayed about it with someone else; the first time he has realised that this business of Christian commitment is not a strange fixation of some whacky Christians but is the key to being a Christian disciple at all. In addition, he has begun to discover how to read the Bible so that it speaks to him; he can make good use of that in his own time with God before you meet again. You have laid the foundation of a devotional life!

Subsequent meetings on a regular basis could profitably cover a range of topics that are essential to Christian life and growth.

The second session

This could major on Christian assurance. It would be good to read 1 John 5:9–21. You would want to get across the truth that if we accept human testimony it is crazy, and very insulting, to doubt God's testimony when he tells us that he has given us eternal life, and that this life is in his Son. 'He who has the Son has life; he who does not have the Son of God does not have life' (v. 12). How black and white it is! You ask your friend, 'Have you received Jesus, God's Son, into your life? He says, 'Yes, I think I have.' In that case, God assures him that he already *has* life that can never end, and he is meant to know it (v. 13). You could point to the further assurance to be found in the experience of answered prayer (v. 15), progressive victory over sin as the Son of God keeps him (v. 18), increasing understanding of Jesus (v. 20) and a determination to keep Christ in the number one slot in life (v. 21).

The third session

This could well be on Bible reading. You might choose Acts 8:26–40, all about Philip and the Ethiopian official. You might have such questions as these in the back of your mind as you try to help Bill to see the power and importance of the Bible in his life: 'What was the traveller doing as he rode along? Why did he need help? How exactly did Philip help him? What might be the modern equivalent of that? What effect did his dawning understanding of God's truth have on the Ethiopian's life? Where does the Holy Spirit come into all this?' Such questions, suitably dispersed throughout your Bible reading time, will certainly help Bill to get to the meat of the passage, and will be a model for the sort of questions he may ask himself during his own times of Bible reading.

The fourth session

This could be on prayer, and one of the most helpful passages in the whole Bible about prayer is Colossians

1:3–14. The questions you want him to reflect on are something like these: 'What are the main things for which Paul thanks God in the lives of these people he had never met? Why is thanksgiving such an important part of prayer? How should we pray for our friends? Paul prays they may know God's power: what sort of things is that power meant to achieve? What are the main marks of Christian discipleship in this passage?'

The fifth session

It is time to do something on the church, the corporate expression of the Christian life. Maybe Romans 12:1–13 would be a good passage to examine. And questions such as these might be in your mind as you ask yourself what important lessons Bill needs to learn about the church from this passage of scripture: 'What does true worship involve? The church is Christ's body on earth: what implications flow from this? How do you see them in your local church? If "each member belongs to all the others" (v. 5) what does this mean for our relationships as Christians? According to Paul, we all have different gifts and abilities. What do you think yours are? Are you using them for the benefit of the Christian community? What practical results are mentioned here as flowing from wholehearted surrender to the Lord? Ask yourself if anything is holding you back from "offering your body as a living sacrifice." '

The sixth session

It is time to look at the issue of temptation and victory. Luke 4:1–13 would be a good passage. And the thoughts you might want to see explored from the text are these: 'What were the temptations that pressed on Jesus? What would they look like in our day? Is there anything significant about the time and place when those temptations struck? Jesus quoted various scriptures when handling these temptations, and this proved highly effective. His quotes come from Deuteronomy 8:3, 6:13, 6:16. What do you learn from that? Have you learned yet to use promises of scripture as weapons against temptation? Don't you think the first and last sentences of this passage highly significant?'

The seventh session

It is high time to look outwards to the whole area of Christian service. A good passage might be Acts 5:40–6:8, and questions like these should prove stimulating: 'What motivated these people to serve the Lord? How about you? How many forms of service are mentioned here? Are the "spiritual" jobs more important than the practical ones? How was it that the disciples "increased rapidly" in Jerusalem? What are you doing now that you might not be doing if you were not a Christian?'

It is impossible to exaggerate the impact which a few sessions of Bible reading like these will have on a new Christian. It will open his eyes to some of the main aspects of the Christian life. It will give him a taste of close Christian fellowship. It will ensure his growth. And it will provide a pattern for his own devotional times and a forum for him to raise questions, and get some answers. Finally, it will be an enormous encouragement to you personally to find yourself able to help your friend to grow in grace and in the knowledge of the Lord and Saviour, Jesus Christ.

9

How about a Bible study group?

Bible study groups are needed

If the Bible is right in regarding Christians as limbs in the body of Christ, it is obvious that we need each other. And this applies as much in the matter of Bible reading as it does in any other aspect of life. If 'each of us belongs to all the others' (Romans 12:5) then we need to find a way of expressing and deepening that interdependence. The Bible study group can be an excellent way. There is real value in sitting with a group of friends and studying a bit of the Bible together, each of you sharing your insights and building one another up. More than that, you share something of your lives and aspirations, disappointments and joys. Room must be made for this human sharing of life and experience, if the group is to 'gel' as a close fellowship of Christians and not just a talk-shop about a book!

You may not feel you could offer leadership in such

a group yourself, but that need not stop you initiating it – members of the group could take it in turn to lead for an evening, so that everyone has a go. After all, it is not as if you are being asked to preach a sermon. You are merely chairing the discussion for an evening among a group of friends.

I was talking recently with George Gallup, the president of the famous Gallup Polls. He told me what he did when he got the idea of a group like this. He called up twelve men he knew and invited them. Ten of them said, 'Yes', and that began the small group involvement which has, over many years, been a great enrichment to his life and that of his friends. It could be the same for you.

Sadly, many churches do not have anything of the kind. Perhaps the minister is suspicious of goings-on among a bunch of amateur Bible readers in a private home when he is not present. Perhaps he feels that Bible teaching should be given by himself in a sermon or a mid-week meeting. For whatever reason, he may discourage small group Bible study. This is a real shame, because it is one of the great ways for people to grow in understanding their faith. And remember, you don't have to ask permission from a minister or anyone else to have such a group in your own home! So why not see if there are people in your neck of the woods who would like to enrich their spiritual diet in this way?

The impact of such a group

There is a massive ignorance of the Bible these days. It is the best-seller that nobody reads. And yet, as we have seen, it has tremendous impact on the character of those who make it the foundation of their lives. I have here on my desk many testimonies to its power. Mr Dzapasi was a witch doctor in Zimbabwe before he landed up in prison. Thanks to the Bible and the personal care of the Prison Fellowship he is now a fully trained pastor. 'It was one day, after the Prison Fellowship members had visited me in my cell and shared the word of God with me, that I was saved,' he said. Before long he started a Bible study group with some of the other prisoners. 'I was even happy to serve my sentence, and actually felt it was not long enough, considering what I had done to God. Prison officers could not believe the change in me, and were astonished when I started preaching the gospel to fellow inmates and even to them!' In the same country a man called Munyoro was awaiting the death sentence, but found peace with God and the comfort of the scriptures. 'The pain and terror of the death sentence was made lighter when I accepted the Messiah as the centre of my life. I began to read the Bible, prayed, and sang to the glory of God.' A Chinese student, Yan Rong Hui, tells how 'God's word was our food during the Cultural Revolution'. Her father was arrested for being in a Christian meeting. All the Bibles in the area were confiscated – but one escaped notice. This was used by many people, her own family included. 'Some of the psalms were copied out for me to read and every day I read some verses. But I asked the Lord to give me a Bible – and he enabled me to procure one from a friend of my mother's. The Bible passages were very useful to our family as we gathered to read them. We had much trouble during the Cultural Revolution, but the word of God gave our family strength to face these troubles and to overcome them.' Enough said. The Bible has enormous life-changing power. We need to read it on our own, but we can also gain immeasurably from reading it with others, and learn from them.

Leading a group

Bad leadership ruins many a group!

The poor leader is often late in starting, has not prepared beforehand and talks too much himself. He cannot restrain the overtalkative or encourage the timid. He asks questions to which the answer is obvious, and then answers them himself! He allows the meeting to drift on far too long, covers only part of the passage, and nothing is summarised, applied or prayed about.

The good leader is unostentatious, asks questions only when discussion dries up, and then very shrewdly and humbly. She keeps to the passage and so avoids waffle. She gently insists on the application of scripture to daily life, and discourages glibness by pressing for further explanation. She defuses argument, keeps the atmosphere sweet and encourages the shy. The good leader is essentially an encourager, who directs operations from the rear. She makes all

the difference to whether the members go away feeling they have had a wasted evening or a fulfilling time of learning and fellowship.

Obviously the leader needs to ensure that there is agreement beforehand about what method of Bible study is to be used and what passage is to be studied. It might be a study course going through a book of the Bible. It might be an examination of what the Bible has to say on an important topic. It might be looking at selected passages. The important thing is that the leader herself is well prepared. There are three vital ingredients in preparation. First, she will need to have prayed about the passage and the people who will be coming. Second, she will need to have soaked herself in the passage (and that will probably have included some commentary work: the New International Version Study Bible is an invaluable ally). And third, she will need to have given some thought as to how she will handle things on the day. She will want to put people at their ease. She will want to cultivate a worshipful attitude. She will want to ensure that all get a chance to participate. She will seek to avoid the dullness of a dry academic discussion, and to encourage the group to apply what they read to their personal lives and maybe to their activities as a group as well.

In point of fact, many of the best groups find that their study together leads to common action for the good of others. They might, for example, be reading chapter 5 in the letter of James about the dangers of wealth and the selfishness it can breed – and decide as a result to go and redecorate the house of an elderly widow nearby. They might be reading some passage in the prophet Micah or Amos about social justice, and this could lead them to make representations before the town council. It is not the responsibility of the leader to come up with ideas like this: they may spring from any member of the group. But the leader will want to ensure that the scripture is applied, and will be open to practical suggestions as to how that can be achieved.

The art of asking questions

Part of the leader's preparation will be to think up suitable questions to help people grapple with the passage or topic under consideration. Good questions stimulate discussion and help people discover important truths that are being overlooked. But questioning is not as simple as it sounds. Here are a few suggestions.

Avoid questions which are obscure, or to which the answer is obvious. Your aim is to open up discussion. It is a good idea to use 'What?' 'How?' or 'Why?' questions. They will probably have more than one answer, and this enables plenty of participation. Don't cap the answer yourself!

Do not be content with scratching the surface. A supplementary question helps, such as, 'What do others think?' or 'What might that mean for us?'

You may find it useful to set one or two questions in advance. This will, of course, involve you in preparing further ahead. But suppose you were studying Matthew 6, two good questions which could prove very fruitful in discussion would be 'What false attitudes does Jesus condemn here?' and

'What attitudes does he advocate?'

If you were looking at the Lord's Prayer, a good question set beforehand might be 'Analyse the Lord's Prayer, and suggest how you can use it as a framework for your own prayers.' Or, if you were looking at the mission of the Twelve in Matthew 9:36–10:20, you could ask, 'What principles in this passage are appropriate (a) only to the apostles (b) to mission outreaches today (c) to the lives of all Christians?'

Be shrewd, humble and focused in your questions. Keep before the group the two questions we have mentioned earlier, 'What did this mean to the original people involved?' and 'If that was the case, how does it apply to us?' In that way you will avoid pious thoughts that have no relation to the real meaning of the passage, on the one hand, and academic observations that have no relation to life, on the other.

The Bible study itself

It is good to start with a meal if possible, in order to allow people to leave behind the pressures of the day, relate to one another and prepare for what is to come. If a meal is impossible, coffee is the next best thing. If you are leading for the evening, it might be good to move next into some worshipful songs, especially if you have an instrumentalist. In any case have some silence before God so that you can all get into the attitude of attentively coming to meet him. You are after much the same thing in the group study as you were in the one-to-one sessions described in the last chapter. You will give a very short introduction, not

parading all the understanding you have gained in your preparation, but keeping it under wraps in case it is needed in the discussion period.

It is important to make it crystal clear how you want the group to proceed. If, for example, you have set them a question or two beforehand, it might be good to say, 'We shall not read the passage tonight, but contribute one by one our reflections on the first question.' Or you might say, 'Let's each try as we look at this passage tonight to find something for the *head*, something for the *heart* and something for the *feet*.' You see, understanding, devotion and practical action should go hand in hand.

If you have decided to do a topical study, such as bringing up children or the use of money, the leader's preparation will be multiplied! But he or she will not parade it: that would inhibit discussion. Instead, the leader will use it to choose particular verses in different parts of the Bible which bear on the subject, and then give each member a slip of paper with a scripture reference on it. They will then look it up, read it out, and the ensuing discussion will be lively and cohesive, because the verses will have been carefully chosen to give a good overview of the Bible's teaching on the matter.

In the discussion let people contribute freely, but you will need to be vigilant. There is always the *over-talkative* member who, in effect, silences many of the others. Do not allow this. It is easy enough to smile graciously and say, 'Good, John, but could we hear from someone else first who hasn't had a chance to chip in yet?', perhaps adding, 'Jean, how does it strike you?'

There are sure to be some *silent* members. It is wise to let them take their time, just sitting and taking it all in. But maybe after a couple of sessions you could draw them out with a judicious question directed to them personally. 'Alf, what did you like most about this passage?'

In a Bible study group composed of long-standing Christians there is a danger of *glibness*, of the parrot-like repetition of Christian technical words like 'eucharist' and 'salvation'. Try to pierce through the religious crust. If, for example, one of the group was commenting on the wickedness of mankind in general, based on Ephesians 2:1, you might gently say, 'That's quite true, Richard, but it also applies to every one of us, doesn't it? I wonder if you would be good enough to change it into the first person and read it to us again?' After a moment's incomprehension he would slowly read, 'As for *me*, *I* was dead in *my* trans-gressions and sins, in which *I* used to live when *I* followed the ways of the world.' At that point glibness tends to evaporate!

Some will be sure to come up with *irrelevant comments*. You want gently to get their noses back into the text so that they are not imposing their own ideas on to it but struggling to uncover what is actually there. Some such question as, 'Yes, William, but what verse do you see that in?' is generally effective.

And then there will be the *mistaken comment*. Rescue anything you can from it, but suggest, 'Does it, I wonder, rather mean . . .? What do others think?'

You are likely to have had an excellent evening. End with prayer, perhaps in the group as a whole, encouraging everyone to utter short prayers or praises.

Maybe, if the group is large, split people up into threes to pray, and have a song or the Lord's Prayer to end with. Sometimes personal needs will have arisen in the discussion and these call for prayer. Sometimes silence is the most fitting response to God's word.

Bible study in small groups can be one of the most effective building blocks of a growing, informed and participatory congregation. It is an opportunity too good to miss.

10

Can I trust the Bible?

As we end this book we need to return to the question we glanced at earlier on. Can I rely on the Bible? If I trust it, will it let me down? What about all the problems I find there? Why should I regard it any more highly than other books? In a word, why regard it as authoritative for my belief and behaviour?

The statements of the Churches

The Churches of the world are almost unanimous in regarding the Bible as the supreme authority in the Christian faith. Of course, church tradition and human reason are also important, but the ultimate authority must go to the scriptures. The Lambeth Conference of Anglican bishops from across the world debated this matter fully in 1958, and came up with this statement,

> The Church is not *over* the Scriptures, but *under* them in the sense that the process of canonisation was not one whereby the Church conferred authority on the books, but one whereby the Church acknowledged them to possess authority. And why? The books were recognised as giving the witness of the

apostles to the life, teaching, death and resurrection of the Lord, and the interpretation by the apostles of these events. To that apostolic teaching the Church must ever bow.

Slightly dated language, but the point is well made. And in theory at least, the Churches do bow to that authority.

The Roman Catholic Church defined its position at the Council of Trent, as follows, 'This Synod, following the example of the ancient fathers, receives and venerates all the books of the Old and New Testament, seeing that one God is the author of both.'

The world-wide Lutheran Church makes much the same claim, in its Formula of Concord: 'The Holy Scriptures alone remain the only judge, rule and standard according to which all dogmas shall be discerned and judged.'

The Presbyterian Churches have as their official statement of belief the Westminster Confession, which states, 'All the books of the Old and New Testament are given by inspiration of God, to be the rule of faith and life.'

The Anglican Church, too, defined its position clearly in the Thirty-Nine Articles. The sixth Article expressly states: 'Holy Scripture containeth all things necessary for salvation: so that whatsoever is not read therein nor may be proved thereby is not to be required of any man that it should be believed as an article of faith.' And even today, despite all sorts of strange beliefs you will find among some clergymen, that remains the Anglican position. Whenever a clergyman moves jobs he has to make a solemn declaration to the congregation of his 'firm and sincere belief' in the 'faith uniquely set forth in the holy Scriptures'. Indeed, no one can be ordained unless, in response to the bishop's question, he can reply, 'I accept the holy Scriptures as revealing all things necessary for eternal salvation through faith in Christ.' The candidate is presented with a New Testament by the bishop, who says, 'Receive this book, as a sign of the authority given you this day to preach and speak God's word to his people. Build them up in his truth and serve them in his name.'

It is plain then that the avowed intention of the universal Church is to give the highest authority to the Bible, believing that it derives from God's self-revelation. Now that is a remarkable claim. Where did it come from?

The attitude of Jesus to the scriptures

Of course, Jesus only had the Old Testament, but his attitude to it is a clear example to us of how we should regard the Bible as a whole.

He studied it carefully, and framed his life in accordance with it

It was in the Old Testament that he saw his role as the Messiah, Son of God, Son of man and Suffering Servant. He realised that his healings, parables, suffering, death and resurrection were all fore-shadowed in those same scriptures, not to mention his virgin birth in Bethlehem. His teaching, too, was rooted in obedience to and fulfilment of the Old

Testament. The Sermon on the Mount makes that very plain.

He regarded it as inspired by God

Jesus saw God himself as the ultimate author behind the human writers. How else can we understand Mark 12:36, 'David himself, speaking by the Holy Spirit, declared . . .'? When rebuking the Sadducees for their unbelief, he says, 'But about the resurrection, have you not read what *God* said to you . . .?', quoting Exodus 3:6. It would be easy to multiply examples of this attitude, such as John 17:12, 'None has been lost except the one doomed to destruction, so that Scripture would be fulfilled', or Matthew 26:54, 'But how then would the Scriptures be fulfilled that say it must happen in this way?' Perhaps the most remarkable example of Jesus' own confidence in the divine origin of scripture comes in Matthew 19:4–5. Here he is quoting the words of Genesis 2:24, which in themselves are a comment passed by the author of Genesis, and Jesus ascribes them to God himself. 'Haven't you read that at the beginning the Creator made them male and female, and said . . .?' Clearly, Jesus regarded this statement by the author of Genesis as nothing less than spoken by God, even though the Genesis account does not directly attribute it to God. The inference is clear. For Jesus a word of scripture was a word of God.

He regarded scripture as absolutely authoritative

In Matthew 5:17–18, the very passage where Jesus goes on to interpret the Old Testament and enlarge on its teaching, he says, 'Do not think that I have come to abolish the Law or the Prophets; I have not come to abolish them but to fulfil them. I tell you the truth, until heaven and earth disappear, not the smallest letter, not the least stroke of a pen, will by any means disappear from the Law until everything is accomplished.'

In controversial discussions with the theologians of his day Jesus would constantly go back to the scriptures for his authority. Was it the question of life after death? To the scripture they must go, and the Sadducees' error lay in their failure to do so (Mark 12:24). Was it a question of what might or might not be done on the sabbath day? To scripture he would go, basing his argument and his practice on biblical precedent (Matthew 12:3–5). His attitude was clear and consistent: 'The Scripture cannot be broken' (John 10:35). The reason was very clear to him. The scriptures embodied God's revelation, and therefore, of course, they were stamped with the authority of God. And although Jesus claimed to embody in his own person the ultimate authority of God, we never find him opposing his own authority to that of scripture. He had not come to destroy but to fulfil. This attitude is found in every strand of his teaching and remained unchanged throughout his life. We find it in his first sermon at Nazareth. We find it in his teaching after the resurrection.

So that is the first and greatest reason why Christians revere the Bible, seek to understand it, obey it and allow their lives to be moulded by it. This was the attitude of their Master, Jesus Christ. It is hard to call Jesus your Lord and at the same time rubbish his attitude to scripture. If he who possessed all knowledge revered it as God's word, so should we.

The intrinsic power of the scriptures

Christians do not treasure the scriptures as normative simply because of what the Churches say or even because that was clearly the attitude of Jesus. They trust the Bible because it works. Time and again in this little book I have quoted people whose whole lives have been changed by the scriptures. Here are one or two more examples to emphasise the point.

David Suchet, the leading Shakespearean actor and title role in *Poirot*, tells how a few years ago he was lying in his bath in an American hotel when he had an impulsive desire to read the Bible. He found a Gideon Bible in his room and started to read the New Testament. As he read, he entrusted his life to Jesus Christ. 'From somewhere I got this desire to read the Bible. That was the most important part of my conversion . . . In the New Testament I suddenly discovered the way that life should be followed.'

Abraham Lincoln maintained, 'All the good from the Saviour of the world is communicated to us through this book. But for this book we could not know right from wrong. All the things desirable to man are in it.' Woodrow Wilson wrote in much the same vein, 'When you have read the Bible you will know it is the word of God because you will have found it the key to your own heart, your own happiness and your own duty.' Stanley Baldwin, a previous

British Prime Minister, observed, 'The Bible is high explosive . . . It has startled the individual soul in ten thousand different places into a new life, a new world, a new faith.' That is what has persuaded so many people of its divine origin. They have read it and sensed its intrinsic authority and inspiration.

The Bible has authority to inform the mind

Ours is an age of vast ignorance about the Christian faith. We need to be informed. And no information is so reliable as the primary sourcebook, the Bible. Ours is an age of unparalleled heresies about the Christian faith. We need to be informed, so that we can stand firm. The Bible provides it. Ours is an age of constant new sects emerging which claim to be true to the Bible and are relying on our remaining uninformed about what the scriptures actually teach. The Bible provides the remedy. Could you lead someone to Christian faith from the scriptures? Could you find the Lord's Prayer or the Ten Commandments? We may be very intelligent and good at our jobs but at the same time very ignorant in this area. Scripture has the authority of a teacher, to dispel our ignorance.

It has authority to touch the conscience

When we read it with an open heart we often feel challenged, rebuked, corrected. It is like a doctor telling us we are overweight or a dentist probing at decay in our tooth. That's the sort of authority it has. And I need it. In this pluralist age where anything goes, in this relativist society where there are no agreed standards, I need an anchor. I need to hear the oracles of

God and allow his word to challenge and change me. Don't you?

It has authority to build character

One of the most remarkable moral phenomena in the twentieth century is the way the scriptures have sustained believers in China, Russia and Cuba, where the most determined efforts, backed up by torture and execution, have been made to change the lifestyles and beliefs of humanity into an ideology devised by the Communist rulers. This has failed miserably. If we wonder how the Christian believers have been able to withstand the immense pressures brought on them, the answer is not hard to find. It has been through the Bible. That has been their most precious possession. They cannot comprehend how little we in the West value it. The toughness and resilience of their character has been formed by this book. And all the might of atheist states has been unable to destroy the church because its faith and practice has been built on the Bible.

I recently came across this fascinating example of the life-changing power of the Bible. A bandit in Latin America captured a colporteur, and ordered him to burn his Bibles. 'May I read a bit before they are burnt?' asked the Christian. The bandit reluctantly agreed, and the colporteur read him 1 Corinthians 13. 'Don't burn that. Give it to me,' said the bandit. Later he read Psalm 23 and the story of the Good Samaritan. The response was the same. As a result, none of the Bibles were destroyed, and in due course the bandit was converted and became a Christian minister. D.L.

Moody was surely right in saying, 'Either sin will keep you from this book or this book will keep you from sin.'

A second story is an equally powerful example of the life-changing power of the Bible. In 1984 Dr Steve Harris, a chiropractor in Houston, who had prayed earnestly for the Lord to use him, gave a copy of the Bible to a difficult and dissolute patient, Bill Last. Six weeks later Last was murdered. A year previously Last's daughter Deborah had been brutally murdered with a pickaxe by Karla Faye Tucker, who was duly convicted of the crime, confined on death row and finally executed in controversial circumstances in February 1988. But while she was in prison the scriptures had led her to a thoroughgoing conversion which made her a blessing to all the prisoners around her. She refused to plead for pardon but faced her death with great peace. Meanwhile in 1990 Ron Carlson, Last's son, found himself idly thumbing through the Bible which Harris had given to his father. Scornful and full of hate at first (for Deborah had virtually brought him up, and was very close to him) he became captured by the power of the Bible's message and became a Christian.

A couple of years later he did the hardest thing in his life – he went to see the imprisoned Karla Faye and told her he forgave her for what she had done to his sister. Together they wept at the feet of the Lord who had accepted them both, and made new people of them. Indeed they became friends, and Carlson petitioned for her reprieve. When that failed, she asked him if he would witness her execution not on behalf of her victim but on her own behalf. Incredibly difficult though that was, he did it, and today he lives in Houston working as a machine operator. He spends his spare time working for the abolition of the death penalty, and ministering to death row inmates. He offers them the new life in Christ to which the scriptures point, a life which can give inner liberation even on death row. How fruitful Steve Harris's gift of a Bible fifteen years earlier has been!

Those are the two main reasons why I, at least, accept the full inspiration and authority of the Bible. First, because Jesus did, and I am his follower. And second, because of the impact it makes on my life, the life of my friends who read it, and the lives of those to whom I spread its message. So may I ask you two questions as I close?

- Will you determine to read the scriptures reverently and expectantly?
- Will you seek to put into practice what you read?

A wise Christian leader was once asked, 'Which is the best translation of the Bible?' He replied, 'The translation into practice.' He was right.